Ground Turkey Recipes

Kristen Carlota

Copyright © 2016 by White Owl Publishing

All rights reserved. No part of this publication may be reproduced, distributed, or transmitted in any form or by any means, including photocopying, recording, or other electronic or mechanical methods, without the prior written permission of the publisher, except in the case of brief quotations embodied in critical reviews and certain other noncommercial uses permitted by copyright law. For permission, direct requests to the publisher, addressed "Attention: Permissions Coordinator," at the address below.

Distribution of this e-book without the prior permission of the author is illegal, and therefore punishable by law.

White Owl Publishing
PO BOX 161865
Miami, FL 33116
info@whiteowlpublishing.com
www.whiteowlpublishing.com

Ordering Information:
Quantity sales: Special discounts are available on quantity purchases by corporations, associations, and others. For details, contact the "Special Sales Department" at the address above.

1st Edition

Disclaimer

Legal Notice: - The author and publisher of this book and the accompanying materials have used their best efforts in preparing the material. The author and publisher make no representation or warranties with respect to the accuracy, applicability, fitness or completeness of the contents of this book. The information contained in this book is strictly for educational purposes. Therefore, if you wish to apply ideas contained in this book, you are taking full responsibility for your actions.

The author and publisher disclaim any warranties (express or implied), merchantability, or fitness for any particular purpose. The author and publisher shall in no event be held liable to any party for any direct, indirect, punitive, special, incidental or other consequential damages arising directly or indirectly from any use of this material, which is provided "as is", and without warranties.

As always, the advice of a competent legal, tax, accounting or other professional should be sought. The author and publisher do not warrant the performance, effectiveness or applicability of any sites listed or linked to in this book. All links are for information purposes only and are not warranted for content, accuracy or any other implied or explicit purpose.

Table of Contents

Table of Contents..4
Introduction..5
Chapter 1: Turkey Burger...................................7
Chapter 2: Black Bean Chili.............................8
Chapter 3: Turkey Meatball Sub...................10
Chapter 4: Turkey Meatloaf...........................11
Chapter 5: Turkey Pizza Casserole...............12
Chapter 6: Turkey Sloppy Joe.......................13
Chapter 7: Ground Turkey Fajita.................14
Chapter 8: Taco Turkey Salad.......................15
Chapter 9: Turkey Picadillo...........................17
Chapter 10: Turkey Vegetable Soup.............18
Chapter 11: Turkey Chorizo Tacos...............19
Chapter 12: Cajun Turkey Pot Pie................20
Chapter 13: Roast Turkey...............................22
Conclusion..25

Introduction

I want to thank you and congratulate you for downloading the book, "**Ground Turkey Recipes**".

Ground turkey has become more and more popular for a wide variety of recipes throughout the kitchens and households in America. However, ground turkey isn't becoming more and more popular purely because of its taste or texture. There are many benefits associated with turkey meat as well that are healthy for your body, which are no doubt one contributor to its rise in popularity. If you choose to begin cooking and preparing meals with ground turkey a major part of the ingredients, than know that you are adding excellent sources of protein and Vitamin B, among other things, to the dinner table for you, and your friends and family.

This e-book is purely designed to introduce you to just a few of the truly wide variety of recipes that you can use ground turkey in, as well as briefly talk about the benefits of turkey meat so that you can better familiarize yourself with the true reasons as to why more and more people are turning to ground turkey as a primary meat ingredient in their meals over other sources such as ground beef.

In the first place, what is ground turkey? Ground turkey is a combination of dark and light turkey meat with the remaining visible fat and skin processed together until a new, ground form is produced from the meat machine. This turkey meat, fat and skin is stripped off of the bone and then further processed until the resulting product has much greater appeal to both existing and potential customers, with good taste and texture. Ground turkey is now highly sought after due to its high availability and less expensive price; however, the most popular form of turkey meat that is bought at the store comes from either legs or thighs rather than from the breast.

But of course, ground turkey meat can't be so sought after just because of the way that it's made, right? One reason for why ground turkey has become so popular is because it is a low fat alternative to ground beef. There are also many other benefits to eating ground turkey. For one thing, turkey is an excellent source of protein, with approximately thirty two grams of protein in just a single four ounce serving of turkey. As a result, turkey is also an excellent source for your body to get amino acids. Think of it this way: by eating just one turkey sandwich, your body will receive nearly all of the daily protein that it requires. If you want to get your protein, there may be no better source to turn to than turkey.

Turkey also provides your body with plenty of Vitamin B. This is because that turkey meat is high in density of Vitamin B; that same turkey sandwich can get you as much as thirty to forty percent of your body's daily required Vitamin B. Not only that, but ground turkey also has less saturated fat. At first glance, this may be a red flag to people since they may think that saturated fat is necessary for the body. Well, they are absolutely right. Saturated fat is above and beyond necessary for the production of hormones, for providing your body with enough energy, and a number of other biological functions. But even though saturated fat is necessary for the body, that doesn't mean that your body needs an over amount of saturated fat. In fact, your body doesn't need an over amount of saturated fat. That turkey sandwich provides fewer than twelve percent of the required daily amount of saturated fat, leaving plenty of room for you to eat other foods and get saturated fat from as well.

So, all of the benefits of ground turkey has made it a recent favorite for recipes in many households. Now it's time for you to get started, and view just a small selection of the many different ground turkey recipes out there.

This book contains proven steps and strategies on how to detoxify your body and enhance your health to higher levels that you've never seen before, and to maintain those levels for the rest of your life.

Thanks again for downloading this book, I hope you enjoy it!

Chapter 1: Turkey Burger

Ingredients:

- 8 oz of Ground Turkey
- 1/4 tsp of salt
- Fresh Ground Black Pepper, to taste
- 1/4 tsp of dried thyme leaves
- ¾ of an ounce of Swiss cheese
- 2 hamburger buns
- 1 tbsp of mayonnaise
- Lettuce
- Onions (preferably sliced)
- Tomato (preferably sliced as well)

Directions:

Begin by pre heating your oven to three hundred and seventy five degrees Fahrenheit, and then placing a grill pan in the oven. Mix together the ground turkey, salt and pepper, thyme leaves, and olive oil until all are well blended together. Then cut the two balls that you can form into a burger. In a few minutes, your oven should be hot. Place the burgers in the grill pan in the oven, and cook both sides for between seven to ten minutes. Top the burger with cheese, and continue to cook until the cheese has been melted. At that point, you can serve each burger on the hamburger bun with the table spoon of mayonnaise, lettuce, tomato and onions. Serve!

Chapter 2: Black Bean Chili

Ingredients:

- 1 tbsp of olive oil
- 2 cloves of sliced garlic
- 1 diced onion
- 1 ½ lb ground turkey meat
- 6 cups of water
- 2 tbsp of chili powder
- 1 tbsp of ground cumin
- 3/4 tbsp of salt
- 1/8 tbsp of ground cinnamon
- 2 cans of black beans
- 3 oz of shredded cheddar cheese
- 1/2 cup of cilantro leaves
- 6 tbsp of sour cream

Directions:

Start by placing the olive oil in a sauce pan set over a medium to high heat. Insert garlic and cook by stirring frequently for a two minute period. Then add the diced onion and continue to cook until the onions have softened. At this point, you can add ground turkey and continue to cook until the turkey has been browned. This entire process shouldn't take any less than ten minutes and no more than fifteen.

Once this process is complete, compile together water, chili powder, ground cumin, salt and pepper, black beans and cinnamon and add them to the pan. Stir until all of these ingredients have been well blended together.

The chili should begin to boil, so you can then reduce the heat to medium to low and the chili will simmer. Keep the temperature at this low heat, continually cook while stirring occasionally for about forty or forty five minutes.

The cooking process is done at this point, and you can top the serving with cheddar cheese, cilantro leaves, and sour cream to your liking. This meal will typically serve six people at a serving size of one and one half cup per person.

Chapter 3: Turkey Meatball Sub

Ingredients:

- 1 lb ground turkey
- 1/2 cup bread crumbs
- 1 tps dried basil
- 1 tps dried oregano
- 1 tps dried parsley
- ½ tsp garlic salt
- ½ cup parmesan cheese (preferably grated)
- One egg
- 2 tbsp of olive oil
- 1 tbsp of steak spice
- One jar of marinara sauce
- Provolone cheese slices
- Buns and sandwich rolls

Directions:

Start by pre heating your oven to four hundred and twenty five degrees. As the oven is heating, combine together the bread crumbs, basic, oregano, garlic salt, parsley, parmesan cheese, steak spice, olive oil, egg, and the ground turkey meat. The meat should be mixed into meatballs that are placed on a cookie sheet that is greased. Bake this for about fifteen minutes.

Cut the buns into two pieces and place them also on a baking tray. Placing the two slices of provolone cheese on the top bun, toast the buns in the oven until they have turned to a golden brown color and the cheese has melted. Warm the marinara sauce in a pan over a low to medium heat, and top the bottom bun with the meatballs. Cover both in the marinara sauce and add the top bun. Ready to serve!

Chapter 4: Turkey Meatloaf

Ingredients:

- Ketchup

- 1/2 onion

- 1 tbsp olive oil

- Ground turkey meat

- ½ cup seasoned bread crumbs

- 1 egg

- 1 tbsp marjoram

- Salt and Pepper

- Worcestershire Sauce

Directions:

As you pre heat your oven to three hundred and fifty degrees Fahrenheit, mix together the Worcestershire sauce with approximately two tbsp. ketchup. Then sauté the onion and olive oil over a low flame until they turn translucent. In another bowl, blend together the ground turkey meat, bread crumbs, onion, a one fourth cup of ketchup, salt and pepper, and marjoram. Shape this combination into a loaf and place it in a baking pan, and apply sauce the top. Do not cover the pan in any way. Bake for approximately one hour, then remove from the oven and let it sit for a few minutes before serving.

Chapter 5: Turkey Pizza Casserole

Ingredients

- 1 Box Spiral Pasta
- 1 lb ground turkey meat
- 1 chopped onion
- 2 cloves garlic
- 1 chopped green bell pepper
- 1 cup pepperoni
- 1/2 can olives
- 16 oz pizza sauce
- ½ cup water
- 1 cup shredded mozzarella cheese

Directions

Spray your crock pot with a non-sticky spray, then in a moderately sized skillet over a medium to high flame, mix the ground turkey meet with the garlic, onion and green bell pepper and cook until the turkey has turned to a brown color. Proceed to wash out the pasta place it in the crock pot with the ground turkey mix. Mix in with olives and pepperoni, and pour pizza sauce and the half cup of water over the mix of noodles. Continue to mix until it has been well stirred, and top with shredded mozzarella. Place the crock pot over a low flame for no less than four and no more than five hours. At that point, it should be ready to serve!

Chapter 6: Turkey Sloppy Joe

Ingredients

- 1 ¼ lb ground turkey meat
- 1 chopped red onion
- 1 red chopped red pepper
- 3 tbsp brown sugar
- 3 tbsp red wine vinegar
- 1 tbsp Worcestershire sauce
- 14 oz of tomato sauce

Directions:

Heat your skillet over a medium to high flame, and cook the ground turkey meat over the skillet until the meat has turned brown. Then add peppers and onions and continue to cook. While this is cooking, make barbecue sauce in a separate bowl by combining together vinegar, grill seasoning, brown sugar, Worcestershire sauce and tomato sauce. As soon as the onions and peppers in the skillet have turned tender, add the barbecue sauce to the skillet, lower the heat of the flame, and cook and let simmer for ten more minutes. Serve up!

Chapter 7: Ground Turkey Fajita

Ingredients

- Vegetable Oil
- 8 oz of ground turkey meat
- 1 chopped sweet onion
- 2 stalks of chopped celery
- 1 chopped green pepper
- 4 oz chopped white mushrooms
- 7 oz of canned tomatoes
- Salt and pepper
- Garlic powder
- Worcestershire sauce
- Parmesan Cheese

Directions:

In your skillet, cook the ground turkey meat over a medium flame until the meat has turned brown. Cook in just enough oil just to cover the bottom of the pan. Once the turkey is almost cooked, add celery and onions to the skillet and continue to cook until they are soft. Season the combination with salt and pepper and garlic powder, then add green pepper and mushrooms until they have turned soft as well. Add tomatoes and Worcestershire sauce for additional flavoring and cook for no more than three minutes, then serve on corn tortillas and sprinkle with parmesan cheese to your liking.

Chapter 8: Taco Turkey Salad

Ingredients:

- Two ears of corn
- 3 corn tortillas
- 3/4 cup of plain yogurt
- 2 limes
- 1/3 cup of cilantro leaves
- 1 ½ tbsp chopped jalapeno peppers
- ½ tsp of salt
- 1 lb ground turkey meat
- 1 tsp chili powder
- 1 tsp ground cumin
- ½ lb lettuce
- 1 cup canned black beans
- 2 tomatoes
- ½ red onion
- 1 small mango

Directions:

Pre heat your oven to three hundred and fifty degrees. As this is going on, fill a sauce pan with water and boil it over a high flame, then add corn as you reduce the heat. Allow the corn to simmer until the kernels are tender. This should take no more than ten minutes and no less than five. Move the corn to a separate plate and allow them to cool off. Remove the kernels from the cob and then place in a separate bowl to set aside.

Next, cut sixteen wedges into the corn tortilla on a baking sheet and bake until they have turned crisp. Turn them once during this process, and then take them out of the oven to cool off. In another separate bowl, mix together yogurt, lime juice, cilantro leaves, salt and pepper, and jalapeno peppers. In another separate skillet, cook the ground turkey meat over a medium heat until the meat color has turned brown. Stir the meat frequently throughout this process, which should take between five to ten minutes. Once the meat has turned to a golden brown, then add in chili powder, more lime juice, and cumin and continue to stir. Then, move this mix to the bowl you will be serving the meal in and put in tomatoes, lettuce, onion, beans, mango, and the corn kernels and tortillas. Make sure that all of the ingredients are mixed together well, and then for the finishing touch add yogurt dressing and serve.

Chapter 9: Turkey Picadillo

Ingredients:

- 3 ½ oz boiled rice
- ¼ tsp salt
- 1 lb ground turkey meat
- ¼ cup raisins
- ¼ tsp dried oregano
- 1/8 tsp ground cumin
- ½ cup water
- 1 tbsp cider vinegar
- 1 tsp drained capers
- 1 tsp olive oil
- 6 oz Goya
- 1 tbsp chopped parsley

Directions:

Prepare the rice as stated in the directions on the package, and then stir in the one eighth of a tea spoon of salt. As the rice is cooking, cook the ground turkey meat in a separate skillet over a medium to high flame until the color of the meat has turned golden brown, and continue to stir over a slightly lower flame until the meat begins to crumble. Stir in one eighth of a tea spoon of salt, oregano, raisins and ground cumin for three minutes, stirring throughout the process. Add in water and continue to stir as you add in cider vinegar, drained capers and olive oil. Cook for five more minutes, and then remove from the flame. Stir in the chopped parsley and serve on top of the rice.

Chapter 10: Turkey Vegetable Soup

Ingredients

- 1 tbsp olive oil

- ½ lb ground turkey meat

- 1 chopped onion

- 1 sliced carrot

- 1 stalk of chopped celery

- 6 cups of chicken broth

- 1/2 cup of barley

- Salt and pepper

- 3 cups of chopped baby spinach

Directions:

Heat the oil in your sauce pan over a medium to high flame, and add ground turkey meat and cook for about five minutes until the turkey meat has turned to a brown color. Break up the meat with a spoon or other utensil throughout the process, and then move the now torn apart turkey meat to a separate plate.

Next, add in carrots, onions and celery to the sauce pan and stir them together as you cook for about three to five minutes. Next, transfer the ground turkey meat to the sauce pan and add in barley and broth seasoned with a three fourths tea spoon of salt and one fourth tea spoon of pepper. Slowly decrease the heat and allow the combination to simmer until the barley is tender. This process should take about half an hour. Stir in the spinach to your liking and it's ready to serve.

Chapter 11: Turkey Chorizo Tacos

Instructions:

- 1 tbsp canola oil

- 1 chopped onion

- 4 oz of chopped Spanish chorizo

- ½ lb of ground turkey meat

- Salt and pepper

- 8 corn tortillas

- Sour Cream

- Sliced Avocado

- Salsa

- Lime

- Fresh cilantro leaves

Directions:

Begin by heating the oil in your skillet over a medium to high flame, and then add in chorizo and onion and cook until the chorizo has turned crisp. This should take about five minutes. Next, add the ground turkey meat to the skillet and season with a 1/2 tsp of salt and a 1/4 tsp of pepper, and then cook as you break up the turkey meat with a spoon or other form of kitchen utensil. Once the turkey meat is no longer pink in the middle, divide the turkey and chorizo combination among the corn tortillas and top it off with avocado slices, sour cream, cilantro leaves, and salsa. Serve with lime wedges and it's ready to serve.

Chapter 12: Cajun Turkey Pot Pie

Ingredients:

Filling

- 5 tbsp unsalted butter
- 3 chopped celery stalks
- 1 1/2 cups white onions
- 1 chopped green pepper
- 2 chopped jalapeno peppers
- 4 cloves minced garlic
- Ground Turkey Meat
- 2 tbsp Cajun seasoning
- Salt and Pepper
- 1/3 cup flour
- 2 1/2 cups turkey stock
- 1 cup dark beer
- 1 cup diced tomatoes

Pie Crust
- 1 1/2 cups flour
- ½ tsp salt
- 3/4 cup unsalted butter
- 4 tbsp ice water

Egg Wash

- 1 egg yolk

- 1 tbsp cream

Directions:

Start out by making the dough to the pie crust. Pulse the salt and flour together in a food processor, and then add chilled utter cubes to the processor and continue to pulse for about five more times. At this point, the dough should look similar to corn meal with some small pieces of butter. You can now add the ice water by a table spoon at a time until the dough turns sticky. Empty out the food processor and transfer to the dough mix to a new, clean surface. Using your hand, flatten out and spread the butter between the layers of flour to slightly crumble the dough. Mold the dough into a shape of your choice, preferably a circular shape, and sprinkle this dough with more flour and wrap up in plastic. Allow the dough to sit for no less than an hour and no more than a couple days, as how it fits to your schedule.

In order to make the filling for the pie, heat oil over a medium to high flame. While this is going on, sauté onions, green and jalapeno peppers, and celery together and stir them often until they turn soft. This should take between five to ten minutes. Then add garlic, ground turkey mat, salt and pepper, and Cajun seasoning. Continue to stir these ingredients well together for a couple more minutes.

Next, bring the stock and beer to a boil in a smaller pot. Add flour over the turkey meat and veggies and mix and stir them well together for another five minutes. As you stir, slowly pour in the beer/stock mixture. This will form a sauce for the turkey, at which point you can add the tomatoes and continue to cook until this mixture thickens up (which should take another five minutes). Pour the filling into a casserole.

Now you can prepare the crust. This can be done by rolling out the door on a floured surface or plate until it is less than a quarter inch thick. Next, you lay out the dough onto the filling and fold the excess dough underneath itself. Use a fork or another kitchen utensil to press the dough against the dish, and cut a one inch sized vent into each pie.

Whisk some egg yolk and cream in a small bowl to make the egg wash. Proceed to use a pastry brush to pain the egg wash on top of the crust, as this will help the crust to brown when it is put in the oven. Bake the pie at four hundred degrees Fahrenheit for half an hour. The pie should be golden brown and the filling bubbling. Cool off the pie to your liking and serve.

Chapter 13: Roast Turkey

Granted, this not exactly a meal that would be exactly suitable for a 'ground turkey' recipe book, but in all honesty no turkey recipe book would be complete without a recipe on how to make a classic roasted thanksgiving turkey.

Ingredients

- 1 turkey (hey, it's a roast turkey for Thanksgiving, right?)
- Lemon Juice
- Salt and pepper
- Melted butter
- Olive oil
- 1/2 peeled onion
- Bunch of celery
- 2 carrots
- Parsley
- Fresh thyme and rosemary

One question that you're probably asking yourself here is how big of a turkey you should buy. Well, that's an excellent question, and it all depends on the number of people you will be serving. A good rule of thumb is that a smaller fifteen pound turkey will feed about a dozen people, a larger eighteen pound turkey will feed about fifteen people, and a big-sized twenty pound (and larger) turkey can easily feed more than twenty people.

Directions:

Before you begin anything, make sure that your turkey is at room temperature before cooking. So if your turkey has been sitting in the refrigerator all day or all night, leave it out in the kitchen at room temperature, but make sure that it is still in its plastic wrapping and that it is placed in a pan. This way, if there is any leakage such as turkey juice that escapes from the plastic wrapping, it will still be entrapped by the pan. Keep in mind to, that if you have bought a frozen turkey, than it will need to be defrosted in the refrigerator for a few days.

If you feel intimidated by the thought of preparing and cooking a turkey, just remember that it's really no different than preparing and cooking a chicken. You still use the same cutting board and kitchen utensils to prevent any potential contamination from spreading to other foods. You will also use the same paper towels to clean up, but different than a chicken, you will also remove anything extra such as the neck or the gizzard.

Now we can get into actually preparing the turkey. Start by pre heating your oven to four hundred degrees Fahrenheit. As the oven is heating, rinse the turkey with water and remove any blemishes such as feather stubs in the skin that you can spot. Dry the turkey with paper towels and lather with lemon juice and salt and pepper.

Place inside the turkey peeled onions, a bunch of parsley, carrots, and celery. If the stuffing appears that it may fall out, you will need to cap the cavity with aluminum foil to prevent the stuffing from falling out and causing any unnecessary inconveniences. To further secure the aluminum foil, close the turkey cavity with a string. The turkey's legs should be close together and held to the body, and the wings should also be held in close as well. Next, rub the outside of the turkey with melted butter and olive oil, and sprinkle more salt and pepper to your liking.

Next, place the turkey breast down on a rack over a roasting pan that is large enough to catch any of the drippings that will result from the turkey. Because the turkey is being held breast down, the skin over the breast meat of the turkey will not become overcooked because the juices from the turkey will fall down alongside the breast. The resulting meat should be tender and tasty. Add fresh thyme and rosemary to the skin of the turkey as necessary.

Now, hopefully you haven't thrown away the inside parts of the turkey such as the heart and the gizzard. If you simmer these in a sauce pan and douse in water with salt for over an hour, it provides good stock for the stuffing.

At last, it's time to stick the turkey where it belongs: in the oven. Be sure to closely follow the directions on the packaging of the turkey, as the time needed to cook turkeys will vary by the turkey (for example, gourmet turkeys typically don't take quite as long to cook as other turkeys). However, a good rule of thumb is to allow fifteen minutes of cooking time for each pound of turkey, assuming that you're cooking at the designated four hundred degrees Fahrenheit. However, over the cooking process of the next few hours you will gradually reduce the intensity of the heat, first to three hundred and fifty degrees and then to two hundred and twenty five. Remember to insert a meat thermometer deep into the turkey breast or thigh to read the temperature. You may want to check the temperature every hour to see how the turkey is coming along. The goal you'll want to reach is one hundred and seventy five degrees for the dark meat and one hundred and sixty give for the white. Remember too, that when you pull the bird out of the oven the temperature of it will actually continue to rise (contrary to what many people may think), so you'll want to pull it out when it's a few degrees short of the desired goal.

Pull the turkey out of the oven and let it rest for roughly a quarter of an hour to let it cool to your liking. Proceed to carve and serve

Conclusion

Thank you again for downloading this book!

Hopefully, this e-book provided you with a decent introduction to the benefits of ground turkey meat and why more and more people are substituting turkey for other red or lean meets in their recipes, and of just a handful of the many different recipes that people are cooking in their kitchens today. Now, you can be one of those people and serve healthy, tasty lunches and dinners on the table or counter for your family. And who knows, maybe you'll come up with some genius recipes yourself.

Finally, if you enjoyed this book, please take the time to share your thoughts and post a review on Amazon. It'd be greatly appreciated!

Bonus: If you leave an HONEST review, email us at info@whiteowlpublishing.com and let us know! We will provide you with a FREE PDF of any one of our ebooks!

Thank you and good luck!

Made in the USA
Lexington, KY
27 September 2016